WORLD OF ANIMALS

SHARKS

BROWN BEAR BOOKS

Published by Brown Bear Books Limited

An imprint of
The Brown Reference Group plc
68 Topstone Road
Redding
Connecticut
06896
USA
www.brownreference.com

© 2006 The Brown Reference Group plc

Library of Congress Cataloging-in-Publication Data available upon request.

ISBN-13: 978-1-84044-224-3
ISBN-10: 1-84044-224-7

Designers: Geoff Ward and Calcium

Editors: Louisa Somerville and Tim Harris

Creative Director: Jeni Child

Children's Publisher: Anne O'Daly

Editorial Director: Lindsey Lowe

Printed in China

Photographic credits:
Front Cover: OSF: Pacific Stock.
Ardea London Ltd: Sarah Fowler 8b, Pat Morris 7tr, Becca Saunders 18, Valerie Taylor 29t; **Corbis:** Jeffrey L. Rotman 17t, 24, Lawson Wood 7tl; **Nature Picture Library:** Brandon Cole 11t, Jurgen Freund 29b, Alan James 9, Bruce Rasner/Rotman 20, 21t, Jeff Rotman 15tl, 15tr, 15b, 23t; **OSF:** Clive Bromhall 3t, David Fleetham 17b, Paul Kay 13b, Pacific Stock 23b; **Photos.com:** 5; **Shutterstock:** Kier Davies 26, Cory Smith 3b, Ximagination 2, 27tl; **Still Pictures:** Kelvin Aitken 19b, Paul Glendell 13t, J. Rotman Photography 11b; **Superstock:** age fotostock 7b, 27tr.

Contents

Any words that appear in the text in bold, **like this**, are explained in the glossary.

What is a Shark?

*Do you think of a shark as a fish with a large **fin** on top, huge jaws, and lots of sharp teeth? Well, some sharks look just like that—but plenty of others don't!*

Sharks come in a variety of sizes, ranging from very small to huge. The male deepwater spined pygmy shark grows to a length of just 7 inches (18 cm)—not much longer than your hand. At the other end of the scale, the largest shark of all is the whale shark, which can grow to 59 feet (about 18 m) in length. Not all sharks have streamlined bodies and blunt snouts. Wobbegong sharks have a flat body and flaps of skin around the mouth. Saw sharks have a long, bladelike snout.

Unlike most animals with a backbone, a shark's ears are on the top of its head! Their pin-sharp hearing picks up sound waves from **prey** more than a mile (1.6 km) away. Small, hair-lined pits, called ampullae of Lorenzini, on their snouts detect tiny bursts of electricity given out by their prey. Special **pores** running along the length of a shark's body pick up movements made by other animals. Sharks also have an excellent sense of smell—they can sniff the blood of a wounded animal 0.3 miles (0.5 km) away. Sharp eyesight

enables them to detect the slightest movement, even in dim light. Most sharks live in the open ocean or in shallow waters near coasts and over **coral reefs**.

At Risk

While attacks by sharks on humans are rare, many sharks are killed by people each year. Sharks are fished for their meat and for the oil in their liver, which is made into soap. The skins are made into purses and handbags. Sharks' teeth are used for jewelry. Today, many shark species are endangered

This sand tiger shark has rows of sharp, spiky teeth. Like many other sharks, it may be killed and its teeth used to make jewelry.

Angel Shark

*The angel shark is so called because its **fins** look like wings. Yet it's a devil in disguise, armed with powerful, lightning-fast jaws and lots of pointed teeth ready to take its **prey** by surprise.*

Angel sharks spend much of their lives hidden under sand or mud on the **seabed**. To breathe, they take in **oxygen** from the water through special **gill slits**, called **spiracles**, on the top of their head. That way, angel sharks avoid taking in sand and mud, too. By pumping water through the spiracles, the sharks can keep still—and well hidden from their prey.

Eye

Spiracle

Pectoral fin, or "wing"

Dorsal fin

Tail

FACT FILE

Common name: angel shark
Scientific name: *Squatina squatina*
Size: can grow up to 20 ft (6 m) long
Key features: flat body with winglike **pectoral fins**; small thorns on snout
Diet: flatfish, rays, and skates; crabs, lobsters, and squid

UP CLOSE

An angel shark's mottled skin provides excellent **camouflage** as it lurks on the seabed. An angel shark cannot swim fast but waits for prey to come close. Then, the shark lunges.

Hidden Danger!

The angel shark likes to rest on the seabed, with its body buried and just the eyes showing. Although the shark keeps still, it is on the alert for prey, which it grabs with its traplike jaws.

An angel shark hunting at night. It relies on camouflage so that it can ambush its prey.

An angel shark's "wings" help it move slowly through the water.

Basking Shark

With its vast gaping jaws, the basking shark looks like a ruthless killer. Yet this huge creature is, in fact, a harmless gentle giant.

Tail

Dorsal fin

Gills

Pectoral fin

The basking shark is found in many of the world's ocean waters. Like the whale shark, it eats huge amounts of the tiny creatures, called **plankton**, that live near the surface of the ocean. A basking shark may sieve as much as a 165-foot (50-m) swimming pool of water each hour through its vast **gill rakers**.

Well Named!

As its name suggests, the basking shark likes to float sluggishly near the warm surface of the water—often with its back exposed—as if the shark were "basking" in the sun.

A basking shark can weigh more than 7,700 lbs (3,500 kg)—as much as a female elephant.

UP CLOSE

A basking shark has about 600 tiny teeth in its upper jaw and 800 in the lower one! When the shark eats it gulps in water. Then it sieves out tiny plankton using its comblike gill rakers.

FACT FILE

Common name: basking shark
Scientific name: *Cetorhinus maximus*
Size: usually around 33 ft (10 m), but may be up to 50 ft (15m)
Key features: huge mouth; skin covered in thick layer of smelly, slimy **mucus**; 5 **gill slits**, inside which are gill rakers for filtering food
Diet: plankton

A basking shark feeds by taking great gulps of water containing millions of tiny plankton.

Bull Shark

The bull shark lives in shallow, muddy water. It lives near humans and is very aggressive. Many people consider it to be the world's most dangerous shark.

The bull shark lives in warm **tropical** and near-tropical oceans and rivers. It prefers shallow waters, including **coral reefs**, rivers, and **estuaries**. This shark has even been found 2,600 miles (4,200 km) up the Amazon River! Although the shark's gigantic mouth is armed with rows of jagged teeth, it is sometimes attacked by crocodiles in the Nile River.

Gills

Dorsal fin

Tail

Huge mouth

Pectoral fin

FACT FILE

Common name: bull shark
Scientific name: *Carcharhinus leucas*
Size: usually less than 11.5 ft (3.5 m)
Key features: stout, sturdy body; blunt head with broad snout; saw-edged teeth in upper jaw
Diet: eats almost anything—turtles, prawns, lobsters, sea urchins, squid, and octopus

UP CLOSE

A bull shark's huge mouth enables the shark to tackle some surprising **prey**. The shark attacks hippopotamuses in the slow-flowing waters of African rivers, as well as antelope and cattle.

Shark Eat Shark!

As well as a wide range of fish and other animals, adult bull sharks eat other sharks. They prey on young lemon sharks, hammerheads, and dog sharks—and even young bull sharks!

A bull shark powers through the water, cruising at a speed of 4 ft (1.2 m) per second.

Dogfish

The dogfish is a shark that might end up on your dinner plate!
It is also called "rock salmon," "grayfish," or "sea sturgeon."
This harmless shark lives in the eastern Atlantic Ocean and
the Mediterranean Sea.

The name "dogfish" comes from the shark's scientific name,
Scyliorhinus. This word means "dog nose." The dogfish's snout
looks a bit like a dog's. However, in spite of its name, the
dogfish is actually a member of the cat shark family! It is
widely fished, including in the waters around the British
Isles. It often ends up on fish-and-chip menus.

Gills

Pectoral fin

Dorsal fin

Spotted body

Tail

FACT FILE

Common name: dogfish
Scientific name: *Scyliorhinus canicula*
Size: up to around 4 ft (1.2 m), but usually smaller
Key features: slim body and slightly flattened head;
large dark eyes and mouth set back from tip of snout
Diet: whelks and clams; prawns and crabs; seahorses,
flatfish, worms, and sea cucumbers

Lurking Low!

The dogfish lurks at the bottom of shallow water, where it usually rests during daylight hours. The fish often hides among rocks. As darkness falls, it sets out in search of food.

UP CLOSE

Like other cat sharks, the dogfish's eyes look like those of a cat.

A pair of dogfish show their spotted bodies.

Great White Shark

The huge great white shark is the perfect hunting machine. Its streamlined body powers through the water. Its amazing supersenses can find victims from more than a mile away.

The great white uses all its senses to track its **prey**. The shark can hear sounds over great distances. It has an amazing sense of smell. A great white can pick up a single drop of blood in an area of water the size of a swimming pool. Close up, the shark sees well even in dim light. And the great white attacks with amazing speed. The first bite takes less than a second!

FACT FILE

Common name: great white shark

Scientific name: Carcharodon carcharias

Size: can grow up to 20 ft (6 m) long

Key features: torpedo-shaped body; sharp, saw-edged teeth; gray and white skin

Diet: fish, including other sharks, turtles, seabirds, dolphins, seals, and sea lions

Dorsal fin

Gray upper body

Tail

Gills

White underside

Teeth

UP CLOSE

Great whites can have 12,000 to 30,000 teeth in their lifetime. The teeth are arranged in rows that work like a conveyor belt. As one tooth wears out, another slides into place.

Shark Attack!

Shark attacks make headlines around the world. Around 100 people are attacked each year, but only about ten of them die. You are more likely to die from a bee sting than a shark attack!

Safe in a metal cage, a diver photographs a massive great white shark.

A great white rears out of the water, showing its fearsome jaws.

Hammerhead Shark

The strange-looking hammerhead shark looks like a creature from a science-fiction movie. The hammer-shaped head helps the shark find its food, even when it's buried in sand.

"Hammer" (head)

Tail

Dorsal fin

Gills

Eye

Pectoral fin

In The Tropics!

Many hammerheads live in **tropical** regions. Some swim in the warm, shallow waters around **coral reefs**, while others prefer the deeper waters of the open sea.

If one hammerhead looks amazing, imagine what a group of 200 or more hammerheads looks like! Scalloped hammerheads (the most common type of hammerhead) swim in groups, called shivers. They gather to mate, but maybe for another reason, too—for safety in numbers to protect themselves against **predators** such as killer whales.

UP CLOSE

Eye

A hammerhead has an eye at each end of its hammer. This gives the shark excellent side vision. However, it can't see ahead. It must sweep its head from side to side to scan the **seabed** for prey.

FACT FILE

Common name: hammerhead shark
Scientific name: Sphyrnuidae
Size: from 3 ft (90 cm) to around 20 ft (6 m)
Key features: T-shaped lobes on head, where eyes and nostrils are located; powerful, muscled body
Diet: bony fish, skates, rays, other sharks (including hammerheads), squid, shellfish, sea snakes

A hammerhead seen from below. Its mouth has rows of jagged teeth for biting its victim.

17

Longnose Saw Shark

The longnose saw shark has a supersnout with amazingly sharp teeth. Mother saw sharks give birth to live babies. The babies are born with their teeth pointing backward so they don't hurt their mother.

The longnose saw shark's snout helps it catch its food. Special **pores** on the snout can pick up weak electrical signals given out by animals, even if they are buried in the sand or mud. Two long whiskers called barbels hang from the shark's jaw. The shark drags its whiskers along the ocean floor. They help the shark find food that is buried there.

"Saw"

Barb

Deep Down!

The longnose saw shark likes to live on the sandy or muddy bottom of the ocean floor. It lives so deep down that it rarely comes into contact with people, so it is considered harmless

A longnose saw shark skims across the ocean floor hunting for animals buried in the sand.

FACT FILE

Common name:
longnose saw shark

Scientific name:
Pristiophorus cirratus

Size: can grow up to 54 in (137 cm) long

Key features: long snout; long, slender body; brown or grayish brown on top, white underside

Diet: mostly eats small fish, squid, and **crustaceans**

Snout

Dorsal fin

Tail

Pectoral fin

Barbel

UP CLOSE

The longnose saw shark uses its snout to uncover animals that are buried in the sand. It swipes its snout from side to side to stun the **prey**. Then the shark bites its victim with rows of sharp, pointed teeth.

A longnose saw shark shows off the whiskery barbels on its snout.

19

Megamouth Shark

In spite of its name, megamouth is not the shark with the largest mouth. That record belongs to the basking shark. But for a fish of its size, the megamouth's mouth is still impressively big.

Until 1976 no one knew that the megamouth shark even existed! But on November 15 of that year a U.S. Navy research vessel caught a 14.6-foot (4.5-m) shark. No one had ever seen a shark like it. This was an historical event because the shark was a new **species**. Since then megamouths have been found in the Atlantic, Indian, and Pacific oceans.

Megamouth's incredible mouth is about 3.3 ft (1 m) across.

On The Move!

Megamouths live at different depths in the sea at different times of the day. They spend the day up to 544 feet (166 m) below the surface. As it gets dark the sharks travel upward, following the shrimp and fish that they eat.

A megamouth on the prowl hopes that small creatures will stray into its gaping jaws.

Pectoral fin

Tail

Dorsal fin

UP CLOSE

The megamouth's huge mouth and tongue are silvery in color. They may even glow in the dark. This may help the shark catch its **prey**. Small fish are drawn toward its huge, lit-up mouth.

FACT FILE

Common name: megamouth shark
Scientific name: Megachasma pelagios
Size: largest female known measured 17 ft (5.2 m); males probably smaller
Key features: huge, rounded head with short snout; enormous mouth with tiny teeth
Diet: mostly shrimp, jellyfish, and other **invertebrates**

Nurse Shark

The nurse shark looks nothing like a nurse, and it doesn't nurse its young! The name may come from the noise it makes as it sucks in food. It sounds like the noise made by a nursing baby.

Nurse sharks are gentle creatures that can be hand fed, stroked, or even ridden! However, they do have a powerful bite. They hardly ever bite humans. But when they do bite, they don't like to let go. This can cause painful injuries. Usually, though, their peaceful nature makes them harmless to people.

Tail

Dorsal fin

Gills

FACT FILE

Common name: nurse shark
Scientific name: *Ginglymostoma cirratum*
Size: around 14 ft (4.3 m); females are slightly larger than males
Key features: gray upper body, white on underside; sloping forehead and short downward-facing mouth
Diet: bottom-dwelling fish, crabs, lobsters, and octopuses

Pectoral fin

Barbel

UP CLOSE

Hanging down from the nurse shark's lower jaw are a pair of thin, fleshy whiskers, called barbels. These are sensitive to touch and taste. The shark uses the barbels to find food.

Resting Together

Nurse sharks hunt at night and spend the day resting in groups on the seafloor, often one on top of the other. They like shallow water and often rest at a depth of just 3 ft (90 cm).

This nurse shark is swimming with one of its babies.

Thresher Shark

With its long swordlike tail, the thresher shark is unmistakable. Thresher sharks are strong and graceful swimmers. They often hunt in small packs.

The thresher shark stuns its **prey** by slapping it with a long tail fin. The shark slaps the water and lashes its tail from side to side. A group of sharks may use their tail fins to round up their victims, which may be **shoals** (groups) of mackerel, herring, or sardines. This makes it easier for the sharks to catch their prey—and they get a bigger meal, too!

A thresher shark's streamlined shape helps it swim quickly through the water.

At The Surface

Thresher sharks mostly stay near the surface of the water and away from coasts. They are strong swimmers and can even leap out of the water. Some kinds can dive to great depths— as deep as 1,640 ft (500 m).

UP CLOSE

The top lobe (part) of the thresher shark's tail is incredibly long—almost as long as the rest of the body. The lower part of the shark's tail is much smaller.

Dorsal fin

Upper lobe of tail

Lower lobe

White belly

Pectoral fin

FACT FILE

Common name: thresher shark
Scientific name: Alopiidae
Size: can grow up to 20 ft (6 m) long
Key features: strong, muscular body; upper part of tail as long as body; gray or black on top with white belly
Diet: mainly fish (including herring, mackerel, and sardines), squid, and **crustaceans** such as crabs

Tiger Shark

With its strong jaws and sharp, jagged teeth the tiger shark is one of the most dangerous of all sharks. It will eat just about anything if it gets the chance.

The tiger shark's nickname is the "garbage can with fins." A tiger shark will eat almost anything—including humans. Turtles, birds, seals, whales, dolphins, cats, and donkeys have all turned up on its menu. The tiger shark also swallows plenty of other stuff too, including bottles, cans, rubber tires, sacks of coal, and even explosives!

A tiger shark's strong teeth can rip through tough shell and bone.

Shark Attack!

Only the great white attacks more people than the tiger shark. But more people die from tiger shark attacks. The tiger shark attacks and saws chunks off its **prey** from the first bite. There is no break between bites, so little chance to escape.

A tiger shark and its baby cruise in shallow waters. If the adult is hungry, it will attack any fish that happen to be passing by.

UP CLOSE

The tiger shark gets its name from the dark bars on its body. They look like the pattern on a tiger. The pattern is strongest on young tiger sharks and fades as the sharks age.

Pectoral fin

Tail

FACT FILE

Common name:
tiger shark

Scientific name:
Galeocerdo cuvier

Size: 10-14 ft (3-4.3 m) long

Key features: broad, blunt snout; large mouth with huge, saw-edged teeth

Diet: eats anything edible; also swallows many other things, such as cloth, bits of metal, rubber tires

Jagged teeth

Dorsal fin

Whale Shark

*The whale shark is the biggest fish in the sea. It can weigh up to 15 tons, which is heavier than three elephants! This huge but harmless giant is a filter feeder, eating tiny fish and **plankton**.*

The whale shark has light spots and stripes on its thick, gray skin. Every whale shark has its own special pattern—like a person's fingerprints. The shark swims slowly through the ocean, only reaching speeds of around 3 miles per hour (5 km/h). When it swims it moves its whole body from side to side. Most sharks just move their tail. In spite of its great size, the whale shark is under threat. People hunt it for its meat, which is first cut into strips and then dried in the sun.

Dorsal fin

Gills

Pectoral fin

Tail

FACT FILE

Common name: whale shark
Scientific name: *Rhincodon typus*
Size: around 39 ft (12 m) but may grow to 59 ft (18 m)
Key features: whalelike body with massive, flat head; enormous gaping mouth with lots of tiny teeth
Diet: plankton, small fish, and other small animals filtered out by the **gill rakers**

The gentle whale shark's huge gaping mouth makes it look fierce.

UP CLOSE

Whale sharks have around 3,000 tiny teeth. The shark does not use its teeth for feeding. This huge shark is a filter feeder. It gulps water into its enormous mouth and sieves out tiny plankton through its gill rakers.

Ocean Giants

Whale sharks are very gentle. Human divers can swim alongside them without fear of being attacked.

Glossary

camouflage A coloring or body shape that helps an animal to blend with and hide in its surroundings.

coral reef A line of coral that lies below the water in warm, shallow seas. Coral is made up of tiny animals.

crustacean An animal with a tough outer shell. Most crustaceans, including lobsters, crabs, and shrimp, live in water.

dorsal fin The triangular-shaped fin on the back of a shark's body. It helps the shark balance as it swims.

estuaries Places where freshwater, such as a river, meets the tide.

fins The winglike parts that stick out from a shark's body. They help the shark swim and balance.

gill rakers Bony parts that sift out food from water passing through the gills of the shark.

gill slits Slits in a shark's body that allow it to breathe underwater. The gills take in oxygen from the water.

invertebrate An animal without a backbone (spine).

mucus A thick, slippery fluid.

oxygen A gas that animals must breathe to survive.

pectoral fin One of a pair of fins that lie just behind a shark's head. The pectoral fins help a shark control direction as it swims.

plankton Tiny animals and other creatures that live near the surface of the ocean.

pore A small opening in an animal's skin.

predator An animal that hunts other animals for food.

prey An animal that is hunted by another animal.

seabed The sandy or muddy bottom of the sea.

shoal A large group of fish.

species A group of animals that share features. Members of the same species can mate and produce young together.

spiracles Small gill slits just behind a shark's head.

tropical The hot parts of Earth nearest to the equator. The equator is an imaginary line around the fattest part of Earth.

Further Resources

Books about sharks

Eyewitness Shark by Miranda MacQuitty, Dorling Kindersley, 2002
Fascinating Facts about Sharks by Jane Walker, Franklin Watts, 2003
My Best Book of Sharks by Claire Llewellyn, Kingfisher Books, 2001
Nature Watch Sharks by Michael Bright, Lorenz Books, 2000
Scary Creatures: Sharks by Penny Clarke, Franklin Watts, 2002

Useful websites

www.kidzone.ws/sharks/index.htm
www.nationalgeographic.com/kids
www.sdnhm.org/kids/sharks
www.amonline.net.au/wild_kids/sharks/index.htm

Index